Simone Biles

by Grace Hansen

Abdo
OLYMPIC BIOGRAPHIES
Kids

abdopublishing.com

Published by Abdo Kids, a division of ABDO, PO Box 398166, Minneapolis, Minnesota 55439.

Copyright © 2017 by Abdo Consulting Group, Inc. International copyrights reserved in all countries. No part of this book may be reproduced in any form without written permission from the publisher.

Printed in the United States of America, North Mankato, Minnesota.

102016

012017

 THIS BOOK CONTAINS RECYCLED MATERIALS

Photo Credits: Alamy, AP Images, Getty Images, iStock, ©Owen Humphreys p.Cover /PA Wire

Production Contributors: Teddy Borth, Jennie Forsberg, Grace Hansen

Design Contributors: Laura Mitchell, Dorothy Toth

Publisher's Cataloging-in-Publication Data

Names: Hansen, Grace, author.

Title: Simone Biles / by Grace Hansen.

Description: Minneapolis, MN : Abdo Kids, 2017. | Series: Olympic
   biographies | Includes bibliographical references and index.

Identifiers: LCCN 2016952609 | ISBN 9781680809466 (lib. bdg.) |
   ISBN 9781680809510 (ebook) | 9781680809565 (Read-to-me-ebook)

Subjects: LCSH: Biles, Simone, 1997- --Juvenile literature. | Women gymnasts--
   United States--Biography--Juvenile literature. | Women Olympic athletes--
   United States--Biography--Juvenile literature. | Olympic Games (31st : 2016 :
   Rio de Janeiro, Brazil)--Juvenile literature.

Classification: DDC 794.44/092 [B]--dc23

LC record available at http://lccn.loc.gov/2016952609

Table of Contents

Early Years

Simone Biles was born
on March 14, 1997 in
Columbus, Ohio. At three,
she moved to Spring, Texas,
to live with her grandparents.
It is near Houston.

Columbus

Spring

5

Biles went on a field trip to

a gymnastics center. The

instructors noticed her abilities.

She was just six years old.

7

Biles started competing
in 2007. By 2013, she was
competing at the **senior elite**
level. She won the **all-around**
US title.

World Champ!

Biles kept on winning! In 2014, she won gold medals in US and world competitions.

11

Biles had a big year in 2015. She won her third straight world **all-around** title. No woman had ever done that before. She also had a record 10 gold medals.

13

Rio!

Biles began **training** for the 2016 Olympics. She and four other women made the US team. The Final Five headed to Rio!

Biles took home the gold in the **all-around**. She also won gold in **vault** and **floor exercise**. She earned bronze on the balance beam.

Together, the Final Five made history. They were the third US women's team to win gold!

Bouncing Biles

At 19 years old, Biles had 17 gold medals. Four of those are Olympic gold. Fans have not seen the last of bouncing Biles!

21

More Facts

- Biles is 4 feet, 9 inches (145 cm) tall. That made her the shortest out of the 555 Olympic athletes in Rio.

- Biles invented and often wins gold with her signature move, "The Biles." The very difficult move involves a double layout flip with a half twist.

- At just 19, Biles was the most decorated United States female gymnast. She had 19 World and Olympic medals combined.

Glossary

all-around – all four events in women's gymnastics, including the vault, uneven bars, balance beam, and floor exercise.

floor exercise – a gymnastics event that can include tumbling lines, several dance elements, turns, and leaps. It is performed to music in a 40 square foot (4 sq m) area and lasts 70 to 90 seconds.

senior elite – a gymnast who is older than 15 and is at the top level of gymnastics, allowing her to compete internationally and in larger competitions.

training – to prepare for athletic competition with a program of diet, exercise, and practice.

vault – a running jump over a vaulting horse, usually finishing with an acrobatic dismount.

Index

abdokids.com

Use this code to log on to abdokids.com and access crafts, games, videos, and more!

Abdo Kids Code:
OSK9466